THE WEIRD WORLD OF PLANTS

▲ A Joshua tree in the Mojave Desert in California.

Plants are some of the most important living things on our planet. Without them there would be very little life on Earth. Animals need them to eat. Plants also make oxygen that animals need to breathe.

Luckily, there are millions of plants to help keep us all alive. Plants cover most of the Earth. That is why Earth has huge green patches on it when astronauts see Earth from space.

▶ This flower, called Sturt's desert pea, blooms in the Australian desert after the winter rain.

Contents

LOOK FOR THE CACTUS

Look for the cactus in boxes like this. Here you will find extra facts, stories, and other interesting information about plants.

▼ **A desert plant called Sturt's desert pea.**

Published by Raintree Steck-Vaughn Publishers, an imprint of Steck-Vaughn Company

Designer: Katrina Fiske
Editors: Jason Hook, Pam Wells
Consultant: Joyce Pope

Library of Congress Cataloging-in-Publication Data
Anna Claybourne.
Plants / Anna Claybourne.
p. cm.
Includes bibliographical references (p.).
Summary: A comprehensive look at plants from different regions, discussing strange shapes, flower power, lethal leaves, tremendous trunks, and more.
ISBN 0-7398-4857-7
1. Plants—Juvenile literature.
[1. Plants.] I. Title. II. Series.

QK49 .G675 2002
580—dc21 2001034941

Printed in Hong Kong.
Bound in the United States.
1 2 3 4 5 6 7 8 9 0 LB 05 04 03 02 01

Acknowledgments
We wish to thank the following individuals and organizations for their help and assistance and for supplying material in their collections: Bruce Coleman Collection 1 (Gerald S Cubitt), 5 top (Alain Compost), 6 (Jane Burton), 7 (Kim Taylor), 11 top (Hans Reinhard), 11 bottom (Jane Burton), 14 (Werner Layer), 20 left (Gerald S Cubitt), 20 right (Fred Bruemmer), 31 (Jane Burton); Corbis front cover (Naturfoto Honal), 2 (Gallo Images), 4 bottom (Gallo Images), 9 bottom (FLPA/Treat Davidson), 15 bottom (Buddy Mays), 16 top (Michael & Patricia Fogden), 18 (Phil Schermeister), 23 (Assignments Photographers), 28 (Wolfgang Kaehler), 30 (Jeremy Horner); MPM Images back cover bottom left (Daniel Rogers), 4 top (Daniel Rogers), 21 top (Daniel Rogers); NHPA back cover bottom right (Image Quest 3-D), 8 (Daniel Heuclin), 10 (Image Quest 3-D), 16 bottom (Stephen Dalton), 19 bottom (Daniel Heuclin), 24 top (Martin Garwood), 25 (GI Bernard), 26 (David Middleton), 29 (John Shaw); Oxford Scientific Films back cover top (Tony Bomford), 3 (Deni Bown), 5 bottom (Rudie H Kuiter), 9 top (Hans Reinhard/Okapia), 12 top (Michael Fogden), 12 bottom (Deni Bown), 13 (Warren Faidley), 15 top (Colin Milkins), 17 (Geoff Kidd), 19 top (JAL Cooke), 21 bottom (Tony Bomford), 22 left (Johan De Meester/Okapia), 22 right (Tim Jackson), 24 bottom (Niall Benvie), 27 (Keren Su).

▶ **Giant water-lily leaves covering a pond. Find out more on page 12.**

WEIRD WILDLIFE

PLANTS

Anna Claybourne

RAINTREE STECK-VAUGHN PUBLISHERS

A Harcourt Company

Austin New York

www.raintreesteckvaughn.com

This plant, called Rafflesia arnoldii, has the largest flowers in the world. They grow up to 3 feet (1 m) across.

LIVING ON LIGHT

Plants suck up water and food from the soil. They also absorb sunlight! A plant's leaves soak up energy from the Sun and turn it into food. This is called photosynthesis.

There are many different kinds of plants. Most of them have the same basic design, with roots, a stem and leaves, needles, or spines. Many have flowers, too.

Unlike animals, most plants cannot move around. They are stuck in one place with their roots in the soil. But their seeds can travel long distances, carried by the wind, by animals, or on water. Plants cannot run away from danger. So they defend themselves with weird weapons, such as thorns or poison.

This strange-looking plant is called a bearded orchid, because it looks a bit like an old man with a beard.

Strange Shapes

▲ This slippery slime is made up of a mixture of water weeds and algae. The algae is giving off bubbles of oxygen.

There are all kinds of weird and wonderful plants, and they can really look very strange. Some plants look more like pebbles or slimy monsters!

If you walked through a desert in South Africa, you would see lots of pebbles. You might think there were no plants at all. In fact, the pebbles are plants! They are plants that look so much like stones that animals are fooled and don't try to eat them.

The green slime found in water is also a kind of plant. It is made up of many plants called algae. Some algae live together in a big, slippery, slimy mass. These algae "monsters" grow so huge they can be seen from space.

Tiny plants called diatoms are a type of algae. They live in water and have hard shells. Each diatom is made up of only one cell. Diatoms are so small, you could fit more than 200 into the period at the end of this sentence.

FOOD FOR WHALES

Millions of tiny plants and creatures float around in the ocean. They are known as plankton and are eaten by whales—the world's biggest animals.

These diatoms form amazing circle shapes.

FLOWER POWER

▶ This is the fruit from a plant from Indonesia called a giant titan arum. It is made of thousands of tiny flowers. The arum blooms only once every seven years.

Most plants have flowers. They can be all sorts of strange shapes and can smell like anything, from perfume to rotting flesh. But most of them do the same job. They make seeds so that new plants can grow.

Flowers need to swap a yellow powder called pollen before they can grow seeds. Grains of pollen are released by one flower and carried by the wind, or an insect, to another flower of the same kind.

Flowers often look bright and smell sweet to attract insects. The insects feed on a sugary juice inside the flower called nectar. This time, insects carry pollen from flower to flower.

◀ **Alpine snowbells are amazing flowers. They give off heat to melt the snow, so that they can grow through it.**

PRICEY PETALS

Rose farmers in Bulgaria have to pick 1,400 flowers to make less than a teaspoonful of rose oil. They sell it around the world to make perfume. The rose oil is so precious that it is more expensive than gold!

When you think of flowers, you probably think of roses and carnations in a flower shop or daisies in a garden. But the parts of broccoli and cauliflower that you eat are also a type of flower. The cones on a pine tree and the sausage-shaped tops of rushes are flowers, too. One of the smelliest flowers is the rafflesia. It stinks of rotting meat.

▶ **You can see grains of pollen all over this bee that is flying from one flower to another.**

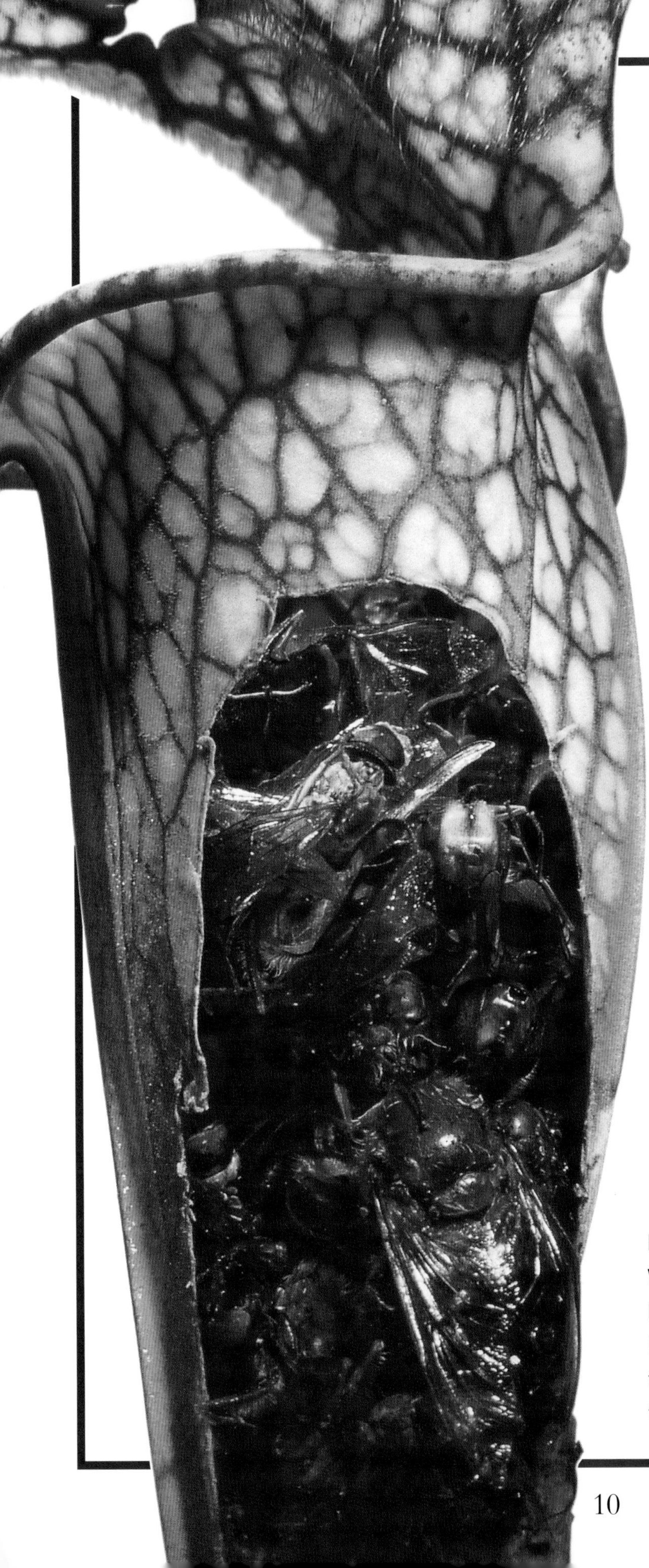

Lethal Leaves

For some plants, water, soil, and sunlight are not enough. They want meat! Most meat-eating plants live in wet, swampy areas. They trap insects, and even small animals such as frogs, for food. Killer plants have weird ways of catching their prey.

The vicious Venus flytrap has deadly leaves, shaped like jaws. Most of the time these jaws are wide open. But if an animal lands on the tiny hairs on the leaves, they snap shut. The victim is trapped inside. Like other killer plants, the Venus flytrap kills its victims with a fluid that turns their bodies into juice.

◀ The pitcher plant's leaves are shaped like a deep jug. Their smell attracts insects. When an insect lands on the slippery leaves, it falls into a harmful liquid in the bottom of the "jug." The liquid turns the insect's body into a juice that the plant sucks up.

The sundew plant has leaves covered with tiny droplets that look like dew glittering in the Sun. In fact, these droplets are a sticky trap. When an insect flies too close, its wings and legs get stuck. The leaf wraps around the insect, and the sundew starts to eat it.

Pitcher plants are really greedy monsters. They can catch several insects at once!

▲ **This unlucky tree is being swamped by a mistletoe plant that sucks food and water from it. However, mistletoe doesn't usually kill its victims.**

TANGLE AND STRANGLE

The strangler fig lives by wrapping itself around another tree and stealing its water and food. It also spreads out its leaves to block the other tree's sunlight. After about 200 years, the strangler's victim dies.

◀ **In this picture, a sticky sundew leaf is starting to curl itself around a trapped fly.**

Tough Stuff

Most plants live outdoors, so they have to be tough. They put up with strong winds, burning sun, heavy rain, and animals that nibble and trod on them. But some plants are not just tough—they are super tough!

A palm tree has a long trunk that bends to help it stay alive. Palms often grow near the sea in hot, tropical countries where there are hurricanes. Winds reach speeds of 298 mph (480 kmh), and many trees are smashed to the ground. But the palm's long trunk just bends in the wind, then stands up again.

◀ These ropelike liana vines are dangling from a rain forest tree.

▼ Giant water-lily pads like these can be over 3 feet (1 m) across.

▲ **These tough tropical palm trees in Florida are bending in hurricane winds.**

ROOT BRUTE

The roots of trees, and sometimes even small weeds, are so strong and tough that they can slowly push their way through pavements. Originally from China, the ailanthus tree grows well in city centers, in spite of pollution. This tree's strength is well known. In fact, its roots can push right through cracks in concrete.

Most rain forest plants grow very big, because they have plenty of warmth, rain, and rich soil to help them grow. The giant water lily lives in lakes in the Amazon jungle. Its leaves are enormous floating pads. They are strong enough to support a child.

Higher up in the rain forest, lianas dangle from the treetops. These are vines with long stems that look like ropes. Liana vines are so strong they can support the weight of several people.

Poison Petals

Some plants use poison to defend themselves. If an animal tastes the plant, it will be sick or even die. Either way, it will not be eating that plant again!

You can tell by its name that deadly nightshade is not a plant to have for dinner. Its black berries taste sweet, but they are full of deadly poison. So are its leaves and roots.

Foxgloves contain a strong poison called digitalis. Eating just a few foxglove flowers can kill you. Strangely, digitalis can also save lives. It is used in very small amounts as a medicine for heart problems.

Deadly Beauty

Deadly nightshade is also known as belladonna, which means "beautiful lady." Italian women used to put tiny amounts of juice from the berries in their eyes because they thought it made them beautiful.

▼ **These pink flowers and shiny berries belong to the poisonous deadly nightshade plant.**

▶ These needles are the poison-filled spikes of a stinging nettle, seen through a microscope.

◀ Poison ivy leaves contain an oil, or a chemical, that can into a rash. Most people have some itching. Some people who are allergic can have blisters, too. The best way not to get it is to stay away from it.

Some plants can poison you even if you do not eat them. A stinging nettle has leaves covered with tiny spikes. At the bottom of each spike is a little bag of poison. When you brush against a nettle, the poison is squeezed out of the bags, up the spikes, and into your skin. Ouch!

Living with Animals

Animals cause lots of problems for plants. They eat them, trample on them, or chew them up and use them to build their homes. But some insects live very happily with plants.

▶ These ants live in a bull's horn acacia tree, which feeds them. In return, they defend the tree by stinging animals that try to eat it.

The bee orchid has a flower that looks like a female bee. This disguise means that lots of male bees visiting the orchid pick up orchid pollen and carry it to the next flower they visit. This helps the orchids to grow their seeds.

◀ Some frogs spend their lives in the tiny pools that form between the branches of rain forest trees.

TREE HOUSES

Plants can provide weird homes for insects and other animals. Some tree frogs live in the branches of rain forest trees, where rain has formed little pools. Some moths spend their whole life living inside a yucca flower.

▶ This bee orchid flower looks like a bee to attract real bees. The bees feed on the flower's nectar and help the orchid by spreading its pollen.

Leaf-cutter ants that live in Texas collect leaves, then chew them up and store them inside their nests. A plant called a fungus grows on these leaves, and the ants look after it and keep it alive. The fungus then provides them with food.

In Africa, another kind of ant lives inside the thorns on the bull's horn acacia tree. This fierce ant bites any caterpillars or other creatures that try to eat the tree's leaves. In return, the tree feeds the ants with a kind of syrup.

Seed Speed

Plants need to spread their seeds around. Otherwise, new plants would grow too close to them, and there would not be enough soil and sunlight to go around. Some plant seeds travel amazing distances.

Plants such as dandelions and milkweed have seeds with fluffy "parachutes," so the wind can carry them. Others store their seeds inside delicious fruit. Animals like birds, bats, and monkeys eat the fruit, then travel with the seeds in their stomachs. After their journey, the seeds fall to the ground in the animals' droppings.

▲ A tumbleweed, or "wind witch," rolling along a road in California.

Wandering Witch

One great traveler is tumbleweed, also called "wind witch." When its seeds are ripe, the tumbleweed breaks free from the soil and the wind blows it away. Each plant scatters up to 250,000 seeds as it tumbles along.

Some seeds have even weirder ways to travel. The squirting cucumber has fruits full of seeds and juice. The fruits sit in the sun getting ripe, then suddenly burst. The juice squirts the seeds up to 18 feet (6 m) away.

Other plants are long-distance travelers. Coconut palms grow by the sea, and their fruits often roll into the water. They can drift thousands of miles on the waves, before washing up on a distant shore.

▲ **A dandelion seed floating along under its fluffy parachute.**

◀ **This coconut floating in the sea has already started to sprout into a new plant.**

Tremendous Trees

Trees are the biggest plants of all, and they live longer than most other plants. Some of them have incredibly tall or wide trunks.

Baobab trees have the fattest trunks of all. They can be up to 98 feet (30 m) around. Baobabs live in dry places and use their fat trunks to store water. Very old baobabs sometimes have hollow trunks, with a space inside as big as a large room.

▲ Baobab trunks contain so much water they are squishy to touch.

▶ Some of the many trunks of a banyan tree.

TREE TREASURES

Believe it or not, jewels can sometimes come from trees. About one in a million coconuts contains a coconut pearl, which is a beautiful round, white bead.

◀ This photo shows people at the bottom of an ancient and enormous sequoia in Lost Grove, Sequoia National Park, California.

The banyan tree has lots of thin trunks. As its branches spread, they put down roots that reach into the soil to form new trunks. A famous banyan tree in India has hundreds of trunks and has spread so wide that 2,000 people can stand under it.

▼ This tree has been blown into a strange shape by the wind.

The biggest trees of all are the redwood and giant sequoia, which grow in the U.S. The tallest redwood is more than 364 feet (111 m) high. That is taller than the Statue of Liberty. The biggest sequoia has a trunk that is 15 times heavier than a blue whale!

FUNKY FUNGUS

Mushrooms, toadstools, and molds are weird plants that are known as fungi. They have no leaves, flowers, fruit, or stems. They grow so fast they seem to appear by magic! Many fungi are poisonous.

▼ Do trees have ears? This one has an ear fungus.

When you see a toadstool, you are only seeing a small part of the fungus. Beneath the soil is a huge tangle of tiny threads. The toadstool that pops up above the soil is like a flower. It releases a simple kind of seeds called spores.

▲ Lichens come in a rainbow of amazing colors. A lichen is made up of a layer of fungus and a layer of algae.

▲ These white truffles may not look very tasty, but they are highly prized for their flavor.

Instead of stems, leaves, and branches, fungi have strange round shapes. The ear fungus grows on rotting wood and looks just like a wrinkled old ear when it is dried. Giant puffballs look like white footballs. You can probably guess what cage fungus, orange-peel fungus, and hoof fungus look like!

The mold that grows on old bread is a fungus. Another kind of fungus can grow between your toes and cause the disease known as athlete's foot. Lichens, which grow on rocks and tree trunks, are made of fungi and algae living together.

TRUFFLE SNUFFLE

A truffle is a delicious mushroom that grows underground near tree roots. Pigs can be trained to sniff truffles out and dig them up. They are sold to restaurants and shops for lots of money.

PLANT POTIONS

Throughout history, people have believed that plants have magical powers. Today, science has proved that some plants can be used as medicines. Scientists are still finding other important uses for plants.

People believe many strange things about plants. Hazel twigs are supposed to be good for finding water. People called water diviners use them to search for underground springs. When they are above water, the hazel twigs are supposed to twitch.

▲ **This plant, called St. John's wort, is sometimes used for depression, or when people feel sad.**

LEAF RELIEF

If you are stung by a stinging nettle, look for a large green dock leaf growing nearby and rub it on the sting. The juice of the dock leaf makes the pain of nettle stings go away.

▶ **Nettles and dock leaves often grow close together, as shown here in this photo.**

Mandrake is a kind of nightshade. It has a root that can sometimes be shaped a bit like a person. This is probably why people have strange beliefs about it. Long ago, people used mandrake to make love potions. They believed that the mandrake screamed when you pulled it out of the ground!

▲ **These old pictures show mandrake roots looking like scary people.**

For hundreds of years, people have used willow bark as a kind of aspirin. Today, oil from the leaves of the eucalyptus tree is used to soothe sore throats. Tea tree oil helps to heal cuts. But the smell of flowers from the lavender plant can help you sleep.

FACTS ABOUT WEIRD PLANTS

▲ This is the world's largest tree. It is a giant sequoia in California. It even has a name—General Sherman.

Here are some amazing facts from the weird world of plants.

Towering tree

The tallest plant in the world is the redwood tree. The biggest redwood alive is 368 feet (112 m) high.

Tiny algae and plants

Some of the smallest plants of all are single-celled algae. The smallest flowering plant, however, is *Wolffia globosa*, which floats on ponds. Each one is less than .04 inch (1 mm) long.

Number one seed

The coconut palm tree has the biggest seeds in the world. They are the size of beach balls and weigh up to 44 pounds (20 kg) each. In spite of being so heavy, they float when they fall into the sea.

Chief leaf

The raffia palm has the longest leaves. They are up to 66 feet (20 m) long, and are thin and feathery. The biggest flat leaves belong to the Amazonian palm. They are nearly 26 feet (8 m) long and are used as sails for small boats.

Mammoth trunks

Some baobab trees have trunks that are 98 feet (30 m) around. Redwoods, giant sequoias, and Montezuma bald cypresses can also have trunks that are nearly as thick.

Hair-raising flower

The rafflesia flower grows up to 3 feet (1 m) wide, and can weigh 24 pounds (11 kg). Its giant, smelly petals are .8 inch (2 cm) thick.

Ancient roots

The world's oldest tree is a bristlecone pine in the western U.S. It is over 9,000 years old. A lichen has been discovered that has been alive for 10,000 years. Scientists have also grown seeds that had been lying in frozen soil for nearly 15,000 years.

Killer beans

The deadliest plant poison is called ricin. It is found in some types of beans, such as castor beans. Ricin is over 10,000 times stronger than the poison of a rattlesnake. An amount the size of a grain of salt could kill a person.

Plenty of plants

Scientists have discovered about 400,000 different types, or species, of plants. New ones are being found all the time. There may be as many as 10 million species of plants altogether.

Weed word

A weed is just a plant that is growing where someone does not want it—such as a thistle growing in a lawn. There is no real difference between a weed and a normal plant.

▼ A forest of fast-growing bamboo in China.

Bamboo shoots

Bamboo, which is a kind of giant grass, can grow over 3 feet (1 m) in a single day.

ANCIENT PLANTS

First seeds

There have been plants on Earth for more than 600 million years. The first plants lived in the sea and had very simple forms. The first land plants appeared about 450 million years ago. They were liverworts and mosses, which you can still find today.

Plant fuel

Coal is dug out of the ground to be burned as fuel. It is made out of the remains of really old plants. Over millions of years, these plants were squashed under mud and rock.

Finding fossils

We can tell a lot about ancient plants from the remains of dead plants trapped inside really old rocks. These are called fossils. Some plant fossils are very detailed. Scientists are able to work out the age of each fossil by working out the age of the rock.

Words About Weird Plants

This glossary explains some of the unusual words you might have seen in this book.

algae (AL-jee)
Simple plants containing only one cell.

aspirin (AS-puh-rin)
A medicine used to cure headaches and other pains. It was first discovered in the bark of willow trees.

attract (uh-TRAKT)
To draw or tempt something toward you. Flowers attract insects with their colors and smells.

botanical (buh-TAN-i-kuhl)
To do with plants. This word comes from another word, botany, which means the study of plants.

cactus (KAK-tuhss)
A kind of plant found in deserts. Cactuses have spines instead of leaves, and they store water in thick stems.

cell (sel)
All living things are made up of tiny parts called cells. Some simple plants contain only one cell, but a tree such as the giant redwood contains billions.

digitalis (di-juh-TAL-us)
A substance found in foxglove. It is a poison, but can be used as a medicine.

fossil (FOSS-uhl)
The remains of a living thing that died a long time ago, which have been trapped inside a rock.

▼ These cup-shaped mushrooms are a type of fungus.

fungus (FUHN-guhss)
A fungus is a strange type of plant with no leaves, such as a mushroom. Some scientists say fungi are not really plants at all!

greenhouse (GREEN-houss)
A building made of glass, for growing plants.

hollow (HOL-oh)
An object that has an empty space inside it, such as a pipe.

hurricanes (HUR-uh-kanez)
Terrible storms with very strong winds. Most hurricanes happen in tropical countries.

nectar (NEK-tur)
A sweet juice found inside flowers. Many insects, such as butterflies, feed on nectar.

oxygen (OK-suh-juhn)
A gas given out by plants. Humans and other animals need to breathe oxygen to stay alive.

photosynthesis (foh-toh-SIN-thuh-siss)
The way plants turn energy from sunlight into food.

plankton (PLANGK-tuhn)
Tiny plants and animals that float in the ocean and provide food for animals such as whales.

▲ **Saguaro cactuses growing in the desert in Arizona, USA.**

pollen (POL-uhn)
A yellow powder made by flowers. Flowers swap pollen with each other to help them make seeds.

rain forest (FOR-ist)
A type of forest that grows in hot, rainy countries.

ripe (ripe)
Fully grown, or ready to be picked and eaten.

species (SPEE-sheez)
A group or type of plant or animal, given a special name by scientists.

spores (sporz)
Tiny, powdery specks that a fungus has instead of seeds.

tropical (TROP-uh-kuhl)
From the tropics, which are hot, stormy parts of the world.

vines (vinez)
Plants with long, thin stems that either grow on things or hang down from them.

water diviner (duh-VINE-ur)
A diviner is someone who tries to find something. Water diviners look for water under the ground.

PROJECTS ABOUT WEIRD PLANTS

The best way to find out more about weird plants is to go and see some in a public garden, or even grow a weird plant at home.

VISIT A GARDEN

Many towns and cities have special gardens called botanical gardens. These are like a zoo for plants. You can visit and look at amazing plants from all over the world. The plants are carefully looked after and kept in the right conditions to make them healthy. There may be a tropical plant-house, with palm trees and giant water lilies, or a desert house with cactuses. You might be able to see Venus flytraps, pebble plants, and rain forest flowers. You can find the nearest botanical gardens by looking in your telephone directory or asking at a tourist information office.

▼ In botanical gardens, tropical plants are kept warm in giant greenhouses which let in lots of light.

KEEP A WEIRD PLANT

If you would like to keep a weird plant at home or in your classroom, try a Venus flytrap. You can buy them at garden centers. Ask for one that eats insects, since not all of them do. Put the plant in a warm, sunny place, inside a glass tank or a fishbowl with a lid. Keep its soil damp with rainwater (not tap water, since Venus flytraps do not like it). Do not give it any plant food. Instead, if you can find them, put a few live ants into the tank. If the plant does not eat them, try feeding it with a tiny bit of raw meat on a pin.

The plant will grow new traps as it gets bigger. Do not feed your Venus flytrap too often. Each trap only works about six times, and each meal feeds the plant for several weeks. Keep a diary of how your Venus flytrap grows and behaves.

DYE A PLANT

To see how plants suck water up their stems, try this experiment. Take a white flower such as a carnation, or a stick of celery with leaves on it, and put it in water that contains a few drops of red food coloring. How long does it take your plant to change color?

WEIRD PLANTS ON THE INTERNET

If you are able to use the Internet, you can go to it to explore the weird world of plants. Remember that websites can change, so if you cannot find all the sites shown below, do not worry. You can find more websites about weird plants by typing in keywords such as "plants" or "trees."

PLANT WEBSITES

Botanical Record-breakers
http://daphne.palomar.edu/wayne/ww0601.htm
Record-breaking plant facts.

Fun Plant Activities
www.gardengatemagazine.com/projects/kid5.html
Information about pollination.

The Garden Helper
www.thegardenhelper.com/flytrap.html
All about Venus flytraps.

Project: Venus Flytrap
www.gardengatemagazine.com/projects/kid5.html
How to keep a Venus flytrap.

◀ **This fly is about to meet its fate between the jaws of the hungry Venus flytrap.**

INDEX